LIVE TO LEARN

AND

LEARN TO LIVE

Tried and True Nuggets of Wisdom

Mirron Noble

3G Publishing, Inc.
Loganville, Ga 30052
www.3gpublishinginc.com
Phone: 1-888-442-9637

First published by 3G Publishing, Inc. April, 2018

ISBN: 9781941247488

Printed in the United States of America

In Memory

I wrote the following poem in memory of my mother who went to be with the Lord in 2006. The title of this book was her life's motto.

My Mother's Hand

One day, her hand, like everyone's, was the hand of a baby delicate and newborn.

But, then one day, as God would have it to be, it became the hand that nurtured me.

But long before it became that hand, God, for that hand, had a very special plan

For she, one day, placed that hand in the hands of the Lord – and he anointed it to be able to speak without words.

That hand during her life, worked diligently, both naturally and spiritually.

That hand cooked meals, took care of the ill, raised a family, gave unselfishly.

That hand was laid on many who were sick. I think God used that hand about as much as he used Moses' stick.

But, one day, again, as God would have it to be, that hand grew old, tired and she became sick.

But, there was something still so very special about that

hand, for as she began to slip away, that hand continued to stand.

When she could no longer speak, that precious anointed hand replaced the strength that had become weak.

That hand now has gone back to its creator and received its reward.

And when it's my time to go too, I'll look for My Mother's Hand to wave me through.

Contents

Dedication

I dedicate this book as a legacy to my five grandchildren from me and my mother, their great-grandmother. I love you all deeply – Spencer III, Jonathan Dewitt, Sarah Elizabeth, Daniel Jacob, and Evelyn Elaine

Foreword

The foundation of this book is based on the memory of my Mother, the late Mother Lottie M. Noble. She was a very wise woman as well as the epitome of strength, kissed by grace! A woman that was crowned with regality and who loved the Lord so much that you could not help but desire to love Him as much by watching her life.

The structure of this book is based on experiences of my own life over the past ten years after going through some major transitions.

When you put the two together, you come out with Tried and True Nuggets of Wisdom that teach you how to Live To Learn and Learn To Live!

Acknowledgment

With Special Thanks:

To my daughter, Stacey Neshon, for her effort and support in helping me to get the book publish-ready. Also, I want to thank her for being the inspiration behind Proverbs "32!"

To God Be The Glory!

Introduction

As you crack open each nugget, you will find an array of treasures inside each one. Some will extract the healing medicine of laughter from inside of you, some will cause a well of tears to gush from your eyes, and some, as you read, will transform into a mirror that reflects your life – where you have been, where you are, and where life is about to take you!

Each nugget, whether a few lines, or a few paragraphs, is a chapter and a story in and of itself that takes you on a treasure hunt. This treasure hunt will teach you lessons that will allow you to discover answers to your questions concerning your life's journey.

These nuggets are a treasure map that will take you exactly where you have been trying to go in life. They will give you the wisdom and motivation to take the shovel of life and excavate, digging deep into life's treasure chest, and come out with what you need to live to learn and learn to live!

PART ONE-LIFE'S LESSONS

Nugget #1
Life's Lessons

Life's lessons are many
Life's lessons teach you plenty

Life's lessons take you to places you never wanted to go
And sometimes keep you there longer than you had
planned to stay

They don't come far and in between
But every day and unexpectedly they show up it seems

Some of life's lessons make you laugh
Some cause you to cry

Then there are others that make you just plain wonder
why!

Why this? Why that? Why me?
Just some of the questions that these lessons bring to
mind.

But one of Life's Lessons that I have learned over and
over again is that Life's Lessons don't always give you
the answers to Life's questions.

But they teach you how to live to learn and learn to live
without knowing the WHY!

Nugget #2
I Survived

More of this and a whole lot of that
I survived

When I thought I wouldn't come out alive
I survived

What did not kill me, made me strong
Trying hard to fit in where I didn't belong
I survived

What I didn't realize is that life comes with its own
survival kit

You have to learn to keep on going and never ever quit

And you will survive!

#Quitters Don't Survive
 #Don't Give Up

Nugget #3
It's Never Too Late

It's never too late to tell hate to wait
When hearts are aching and love ties are breaking

It's never too late to tell fear that he's no longer welcome to stay
So pack up your bags and go on your way

It's never too late to command depression to halt
Because he's done enough harm; it's time for him to move on

It's never too late to stop unforgiveness in his tracks
And let him know that he must go back

Because you have decided that he's not worth holding on to
Free yourself and become a better you

It's never too late
Whether many or few
To get rid of whatever is hindering you!

#Bye Bye

Nugget #4
The Benefits of Wisdom

I have thought long and hard about a nugget of wisdom that I often heard my Mother say. "You prepare for war in time of peace!"

It is such a power-packed nugget; yet for a long time, seemingly, I could not crack open this nugget and extract the real meat of it.

I do not know the origin or history of this quote. I haven't even taken the time to do any research in order to find out its source. All I know is that I heard my Mother say it countless times throughout her lifetime.

But just recently as I began to write this, a nugget dropped into my spirit concerning this nugget! I purposely did not do any research or googling because I did not want to be influenced by facts over wisdom.

Simply put, this statement is loaded with wisdom. So much so that it will spill over onto any situation, circumstance, or season of your life.

Whether what you are dealing with or facing is for a season, a reason, or a lifetime, this nugget of wisdom, if you apply it, will benefit you GREATLY!

It is one of those all-purpose, cure-all remedies for life's challenges and battles of all kinds that will guarantee you great results if used wisely and properly!

And I must say that my Mother was tried and true proof that this remedy of wisdom truly works!

This remedy has many benefits as well as side-effects so use caution when you apply this nugget of wisdom.

If you follow the instructions carefully, even the side effects will give you amazing results so beware of becoming a much stronger individual as you engage in war on the front lines of life's battles!

Last but not least, you will become so much wiser for it all!

Try It, It Really Works!
– GUARANTEED –

Harsh realities, rude awakenings, burning the midnight oil with the fuel of prayers and more prayers.

And Life Goes On!

Fears watered with tears, disappointments that grow like weeds. God knows another heartache is not what we need.

And Life Goes On!

Burdens to bear even though God is always there. Sleepless nights, no relief in sight.

And Life Goes On!

Trouble and tribulations spending the night uninvited, and they don't pack up and leave when the sun comes up.

And Life Goes On!

And life goes on because there are lights at the end of every dark tunnel, rainbows after the storms, joy of the birth of a newborn after someone has passed on.

And life goes on because there are healings after sickness, miracles after miseries…and so much more of life that we would miss if life did not go on.

So Life Goes On!

Nugget #6
Can You Afford

Can you afford to speak that last word
That was best left unheard?

Is it necessary to always say what's on your mind
That could hurt someone's feeling
That was so unkind?

Was it really worth it to lose someone's respect in order
to have your way?
Can you afford the price that you will later pay!

#You Reap What You Sow
#Be Kind To Others

Nugget #7
Take It Back

Take your mind back to where you first believed
That anything you wanted, you could achieve

Take your heart back to the place where it was over-
whelmed with love,
So thankful for every little blessing that was sent from
above

Take your soul back to where it cried out and longed
more for the Heavenly Master
To bring you through all of life's disasters

Take your mind, heart, and soul back to their rightful
place
And remain there and receive HIS Grace!

#By God's Grace You Will Make It

Nugget #8
It's A Caterpillar...It's A Butterfly...IT'S ME!

What do all of these very unique creatures have in common? Time! It takes time to grow, transform, or metamorphose into an absolutely outstanding product.

While these changes are taking place over time, you will find yourself living to learn and learning to live – forever learning from the womb to the tomb.

Whether voluntary or involuntary, you will discover that life starts off as a book of blank pages, and with every experience it becomes filled with lessons learned over whatever time God sees fit to allow you to live on this earth.

When we first enter into this world and that first burst of air fills our lungs, we begin our learning journey. Learning to cry becomes our first of many and countless lessons.

As we shed tears, we learn that crying is not only an emotional overflow due to hurt or some kind of pain, but it is also a language – a language sometimes foreign even to oneself even though we may speak it fluently and frequently!

But, in spite of the fact that this language is mostly spoken from a place of pain, it can also be spoken when we are visiting a place of joy, peace, and love.

There are times when we simply cannot wrap our brains around the fact that we can actually speak this language while we are visiting such contrasting places.

So, whatever the place life allows us to visit, God has given us a language that does not require an academic lesson to learn. This language flows like a mighty river from the depths of lessons that we have learned over time that teaches us tried and true nuggets of life!

And just remember that the creator of this language understands every drop, and when we are transitioning from season to season in our lives, we are assured that He recognizes that It's ME! Because my tears speak a language that only He understands. He knows me by my tears and He understands that sometimes I need a little bit more time to become all that He created me to be!

It's a Caterpillar…It's A Butterfly…It's Me!

Nugget #9
A Change Is Coming

A change is coming, wait patiently and see.
What is today, tomorrow will no longer be.

Just as sure as the name of the day will change
Your present condition won't remain the same.

There is an expiration date and it won't be late.

Just as sure as you went in, you will come out –
A changed person without a doubt!

#Nothing Remains The Same But Jesus
#Jesus Can Change Your Circumstances

Nugget #10
Close The Door

Close the door if you can't take it anymore

On whatever is robbing you of your peace and joy.

Then lock it behind you and throw away the key.

Tell yourself this shall no longer be.

You made a mistake and let it in.

But you've learned your lesson, now don't do it again!

Nugget #11
Take A Walk

Take a walk on the kind side of life's street
And give a smile to everyone you may happen to meet.

Whether they return that smile or not
You just continue to take a walk.
You see chances are you will pass that way again
And someone you met before, who did not return your
smile, will remember when

You passed them by and gave them a smile
That made their journey so much more worthwhile!

#Kindness Is Good Exercise

Nugget #12
Hurting For Someone Else

When you are wounded, I bleed.
When you are without, I have a need.

When you are lonely, I feel the same.
When you are hurting, it becomes my pain.

You wonder why it is this way –
Because I've already been where you are today!

#We Bear One Another's Burdens

Nugget #13
If You Live Long Enough

If you live long enough, you will find yourself wishing you knew then what you know now!

If you live long enough, you will wish you had waited to do some of the things that you have already done!

If you live long enough, you will regret that you did not do a lot of things differently!

If you live long enough, you will come to understand some things that you once didn't have a clue about!

So, live each day of the remainder of your life as if you know how much longer you have to live...and by the grace of God, if you live long enough, you will end up just where you want to be!

****

Now I know what my mother meant when she would always say, "If you live long enough."

I HAVE LIVED LONG ENOUGH!

Nugget #14
Blessed To Be A Blessing

It doesn't take a whole lot. You always have more than you think you do, and you always have something that is just what someone else needs.

Don't you know that your blessings are seasonal? So when you are being abundantly blessed, the overflow is not for you but for you to be a blessing to someone else. And remember that the more you give and are a blessing, the more you will receive.

Peace becomes a blessing to someone who is buried beneath confusion and unrest. Love becomes a blessing to someone who is cast down with rejection and heartbreak.

So, when you are walking in your season of blessings of any kind, remember that you are being blessed to be a blessing.

#Helping Someone Else Becomes A Blessing To You

Nugget #15
Made to Believe

Throughout our lives we were made to believe that whatever we were taught was the way things were meant to be.

But now I know that I was made by my Creator to believe that all things are possible to them that believe!

Nugget #16
Now I See

Now I see.
Things are no longer cloudy.

I used to think that relief was not near
But later realized that it was closer than it appeared.

Now I can see what I couldn't see before –
That my God sees and my God knows!

#I Can See Clearly Now

Nugget #17
Tough Love

Tough love has a way of teaching you the best way
to love. Sometimes the best way to love is from afar.
Keep loving, but at the same time keep your distance.
It may be tough at first but eventually you will get used
to it, and it will happen automatically!

Nugget #18
When Your Plans Fail

When your plans fail and it seems like there is nothing
left for you to do

That means that God has something much greater pre-
pared for you.

He never intended for you to make your own plans so
He waited purposely for yours to fail

So that you would come to realize that without Him
you cannot prevail!

Nugget #19
Going Through To Get Through

We often complain and play the blame game
About life being so hard

If it ain't one thing, it's another
At times it seems impossible to go further

We dread the going through
But we love the coming out

But one thing I have come to know
Without a doubt

That going through makes us stronger and stronger to
get through to the other side!

Nugget #20
Hugs and Kisses

There is something healing about Hugs and Kisses.
If you haven't given or received one lately, you don't
know what you are missing.

Something as simple as a peck on the cheek
Or a tiny or big hug will strengthen you whenever you
are weak.

So, hug and kiss more!

#Medicine Is In A Kiss And A Hug
#A Little Goes A Long Way

Nugget #21
Substitutions

Substitutions are the birth parents of procrastination. Procrastination is a troublemaker who will off-center every divine plan and perfect will of God for your life.

Procrastination causes you not to react and respond timely to the bidding and word of God. Then you end up in the permissive will of God which breeds problems that were never intended for you!

This family of troublemakers will cause you to waste precious time trying to fix things that are not broken.

Jesus is the way! There is no need for a substitution or any further procrastination!

This family is just a bunch of sluggards and under-achievers that will cause you to be just as dysfunctional as they are, if you allow them.

Nugget #22
Finishing Strong

Many have and will enter the race of life. Some have finished, some will finish, but how many will finish strong?

Those who finish strong are not ashamed to admit
That at times they just plain wanted to quit.

They will confess that oftentimes they were extremely weak
And fell helplessly at the Savior's feet.

They that finish strong think it not robbery to suffer long
Or even yield their rights so that someone else won't go wrong.

They realized that there is a cross that we all must bear
And they are willing to follow Christ any and everywhere.

They are not afraid to ask for help
Or to admit that they struggle while going through a test

Because before they started, they made up their minds
That whatever it takes they would make it to the finishing line!

#Strength Starts In The Mind
#Exercise Your Mind Muscle In The Word Of God
#Be Strong In The Lord

Nugget #23
Listen!

Learning to listen is not an easy lesson
Because most of the time we are too busy talking and
asking questions.

So do yourself a favor and give your mouth a rest.
Let your ears do all the work, and you will pass more of
life's tests!

Nugget #24
In The Midst Of The Storm

In the midst of life's storms
There is so much that you can learn

About what you are able to endure
Because of what is inside of you

You will be blessed and amazed to know
Just how much you will grow
In the midst of the storm!

Nugget #25
Divorce

My sister or brother, have you been through a divorce
That left you thinking, "Oh my God, can it get any
worse?"

I am here to give you some advice
Believe me, I know, I've been there twice

Truly the end is just the beginning
Just give God time to heal you and then move on and
enjoy your new season

Be grateful that you survived the summer season of
your life
Even though circumstances of the divorce sometimes
got very hot
And you weren't sure if you would make it out or not

The fall and winter finally passed over
It's now time to spring back and recover

Ah! But there's one more season waiting for you
This season my friend is called DUE!

Nugget #26
Pick Your Battles

You have to learn in life to pick your battles
For some are not worth the fight

Remember the biggest battle is inside of you
Fighting to do what is right!

Nugget #27
Speak Wisdom

*Based On A True Story

Whenever there is a life convention in town where Knowledge, Experience, and Wisdom are speaking, Common Sense makes it his business to be there.

When Knowledge approaches the stage preparing to speak, Common Sense takes out his pen and pad and prepares to take notes and receive a wealth of information.

When Experience is announced, Common Sense applauds loudly, excitedly anticipating a profound presentation.

But when Wisdom is making his speech, Common Sense sits on the edge of his seat very quietly and still, as if he is glued to it. He hangs onto and soaks up every word that comes out of Wisdom's mouth and doesn't even write down a single note. You can tell that he is absolutely mesmerized by what Wisdom has to say.

He leaves there inspired, motivated, and most of all ready to apply everything that Wisdom has said. Common Sense declares that Wisdom is the best speaker ever and that everyone should go and hear him at least once in their lifetime!

Nugget #28
Lost In the Battle

As I look back over the battlefield of life, I realize that there were so many casualties. There was so much that was lost but not without a cost!

I lost my ability to see defeat in the battle...but after recovery I discovered that I had gained vision. I could not only see what I could not see before the battle, but I had a vision of myself never returning to where I wasn't wanted or even no longer desired to be!

Before I went into battle, I was "sooo" afraid of how things would turn out in my life, but somewhere in the struggle I lost all of my fears of the unknown!

At some point I looked back and saw a trail of blood that had been lost in the battle, and I panicked because of the amount of the blood. I cried out, "Oh God, I have lost so much blood in these battles!"
But then God spoke back to me and said, "The battles were not yours, they were mine. And the blood is the blood that I shed for you on Calvary when I died on the cross...YOU WERE COVERED BY THE BLOOD THAT I SHED IN THE BATTLE!"

#The Blood Of Jesus Never Loses Its Power

Nugget #29
Red Flags

Red flags do not always come in the color red. If it is a red flag, it is always there. But, many times we fail to recognize it by choosing to become color blind, or we just plain ignore it.

Oftentimes, red flags will speak to our hearts and tell us to slow down and proceed with caution. But just know that when this is coming from a red flag, you are NOT to slow down and proceed with caution. Instead you are to STOP! It is still a red flag. Don't ignore it. Wait for God's green light before you go full speed ahead!

#Don't Ignore
#Red Flags Always Mean STOP

D O N' T   I – Intentionally
G – Going
N – Nowhere
O – Overlooking
R – Real
E – Evidence

Bits and pieces of my life were once everywhere.
Bits of it over here
And a whole lot of pieces over there

One piece of my mind
Was hard to find
Because I had given it away
When I had too much to say

Bits of my heart
Had been ripped apart
Because I had put too much love and trust where it
wasn't deserved

Then one day I decided to gather up all the bits and
pieces
And me, myself, and I had a meeting

Yes, it was time to get it all together
Because I needed all the bits and pieces to make my life
better!

Nugget #31
Relationships

A relationship is a match made in heaven between friendship and love. They make such a lovely couple, and they are so much better together.

When friendship and love hook up, there is nothing they can't conquer. Together they overcome loneliness, sickness, trouble of all kinds…you name it, and a good relationship will help you get through it.

So when God puts those two together, nothing or no one can put them asunder!

Nugget #32
Only God Can Do It

There are some things in life that God allows us to do on our own.
He steps aside and leaves us alone.

All we have to do to make the right choice
Is to listen attentively to His voice.

Then there are other things that Only God Can Do
And we have no choice in the matter.
If we step aside and leave Him alone,
We will come out much better and happier!

Nugget #33
Life Hackers

Let me warn you about life hackers.
When we least expect it, they will attack us.

They come to rob you of your identity
So that you won't become what you're supposed to be.

But you can report them to the Lord in prayer,
And you shall recover all that they took from you!

#Prayer Will Make Sure You Recover All That The Enemy Has Stolen From You

#Pray Without Ceasing

Nugget #34
Wash Your Hands

Wash your hands of everything that you don't understand,
And prepare to partake of bigger and better plans.

It's time to start your life over with a clean slate
Can't keep crying over spilled milk and dirty mistakes.

So, wash your hands of all the regrets
Because you can't touch God's blessings with hands
soiled with anger and bitterness!

Nugget #35
Speak Your Day

Do you not know that you have the power to speak your day?

Things in your life will react and appear according to what you say.

And even if you don't see it right away

Just keep saying it until you see it.

Without a doubt, it's not a denial, only a delay!

Nugget #36
I Tried

There were times when I tried to give up but to no avail.

Something deep inside of me said,
You can make it, just keep pressing ahead.

I tried to throw up my hands and say,
I don't think I can do this another day.

I tried and I tried not to shed another tear
At the same time trying to figure out my real purpose for being here.

Then one day I decided to try to no longer try to quit.

Instead I tried and I tried to succeed, and if I failed, I tried again!

Nugget #37
You Never Know

You never know which way life's road will go

Sometimes it will take a turn for the worse

And then you never know, it may just take you on a more interesting and exciting course

It may take you straight to a brighter day

Or you could just as well end up somewhere you don't want to stay

So, wherever life may take you, try your best to enjoy the trip

Because you never know what's around the next corner!

Nugget #38
I Don't Care

I don't care what you say
I'm moving on anyway

I don't care what you see
You've only seen one side of me

I don't care what you are thinking
I'm going to pick up the pieces and start mending

I don't care what you know
I might can't tell you but I can sure show you

I don't care what you say, see, think, or know
Because I'm not that same person that I was before!

#moving on

Nugget #39
Tell Someone Thanks

You need to take the time to say thanks to someone
who prayed for you

For if it wasn't for their prayers, it would have been
much harder for you to push through

Thank them for all the time that they spent on their
knees

Crying out to the Father in Heaven asking Him to help
you please

You just may need them to pray for you again

And to stand in the gap until the victory you win

It will encourage them to know

That the prayers that they prayed were answered and
opened Heaven's door

So, when you tell God thank you

Tell someone who prayed thanks too!

Nugget #40
Yes I Will

Yes I can, oh yes I will
Let God fight my battles while I keep still

Yes I will not say a word
I don't always have to speak in order to be heard

Yes I will get up and continue to stand
After being knocked down over and over again

Yes I will fulfill my purpose and destiny
Because I have my God on my side and He promised
never to leave or forsake me!

Nugget #41
When I Wake Up

When I wake up I always have God on my mind

And He always greets me with the biggest smile of a bright sunshine

He blesses me with the gift of a brand-new day

Along with life, health, and strength to get started on my way

Over the years when I wake up I have come to know

That my love for Him I must first surely show

For He has done so much for me

Just for waking me up, I owe Him eternally!

Nugget #42
You Can Try

You can try but I promise you that you won't succeed

At missing the mark if you stay on your knees

Pray in the morning, noon, and night

You can try this and I promise you will win every fight

This recipe works for all of life's ills

I found it to be better than any old doctor's pills

You can try it for yourself and see

It certainly has done wonders and miracles for me

It won't cost you a single dime

Just takes a little every day of your time!

Nugget #43
Healing

Healing of any kind is a process. It takes time. Some healings take longer than others but this is not a bad thing. The longer the process takes is an indication that God is taking His time with you. He does not put new wine into old bottles.

The aging of the process is for the purpose of making you a brand-new vessel that is fit for His use. You have been crushed by what you have gone through! God is giving you time to bleed every drop of the oil of His anointing. He then takes it and saturates your wounds with new power, strength, and abilities.

The main thing for you to do is to rest in His care and do not become frustrated with the process and attempt to find a shortcut to your healing!

Healing is a process that takes God's time for you to fully recover and become not just healed but whole!

Nugget #44
The Best Is Yet To Come

The Best is yet to come no matter what you have been through or where you've come from

Something so exciting fresh and brand new is coming even if it's not yet in view

But don't you fret if it's not Good now or doesn't seem to be getting any Better because

The Best Is Yet To Come!

#Good, Better, And Then The Best
#Saving The Best For Last

PART TWO - Wisdom Nuggets For The Soul

Nugget #45
Provisions

Grains and wholesome wheat
That grow abundantly for us to eat

Are just a few of the many provisions of our Creator

A hearty and hefty smile
That lasts a while
From a stranger that crosses your path

Is another provision that quenches a thirsty and hungry
need

A hug we take for granted
A kiss on the cheek planted

Little things that make a BIG difference
Provide lasting and healing memories for the soul!

Nugget #46
The Well Is Not Dry

The well will never become dry
As long as you and I continue to cry

For those lost souls that are drowning
And in need of Jesus' blood-filled fountain

The well of salvation flows abundantly and freely
We draw for lost souls when we are interceding!

#Stand In The Gap For Others

Nugget #47
Healing Without Scars

Healing without scars means you are not just healed
but whole. Healing without scars means that not only
have you forgiven but you have forgotten. Healing
without scars means you are ready to move on with
your life. Healing without scars means you don't look
like what you have been through. Healing without
scars means that you are going to be just fine. Healing
without scars means that you have lived to learn and are
learning to live!

#Thank You Lord For Your Healing Power!

Nugget #48
More To Come

There's more to come and then some

For your prayers and fastings
Something that will blow your mind is about to happen

For all the good seeds that you have sowed
You're going to reap the overflow

For all the tears that you have shed
A river flowing with blessings is on the way

Nothing that you have been through will be wasted

There's more to come of God's manifold blessings!

Nugget #49
Don't Underestimate

Don't underestimate the power of love
Or the Heavenly Father who sent it from above

Don't underestimate the power of a sacrifice
Or the Son of God who gave His Life

Don't underestimate the freedom that you have received
To live the life in which you believe

Don't underestimate the blessings that you have been given
so that you can be a blessing!

Nugget #50
Dreams

Dreams are such an awesome wonder, it seems

Far beyond what you can imagine or think

I dream, you dream, all of God's children dream

Now the meaning of dreams
That's an entirely different thing

From some you never want to awake
Then there are others that really disturb us

Some dreams cause us to ponder and wonder
Nowhere to turn but to God in prayer

A mystery only He knows
So, I close my eyes and pray for sweet dreams again!

Nugget #51
You Can Dream Again

You can and will dream again
It's not over yet, if you know what I mean

God knew you needed time to heal from the past
He's been saving the very best of your life for last

So, day or night you will dream again
And you will begin to see things in your life become
better than they have ever been!

#sweet dreams

Nugget #52
On The Run

Run for your crown of life.

Run because the enemy is after you, and he is looking for you to give up and turn yourself in.

He doesn't know that you are covered by the Blood of Jesus Christ

Even though he has sent his search party out looking for you more than once or twice

So, he might as well call his search party off because I'm on the run for LIFE Eternal.

You see I am an Escapee!

What about you?

#Run, Don't Look Back

Nugget #53
The End From The Beginning

I know your end from the beginning,
Says the Lord to me and you

Before I placed you in your mother's womb
I already knew all the things that you were put on this
earth to do

He planned our lives carefully
All things were to work together for our good

Even though sometimes we messed up in between
By not doing what we should

But He also knew this too from the beginning
So, He worked it in His perfect will

That's why He sent His son to die for us
Up on Calvary's Hill!

Nugget #54
It Only Takes A Moment

It only takes a moment for everything to go up in smoke

It only takes a moment for a heavy rain to wash away all the results

In a moment in the twinkling of an eye, eternity will begin

So, make every temporal moment count

It only takes a moment for this life to end!

#Jesus Is Soon To Come

Nugget #55
It Could Have Been Me

It could have been me who refused to obey God

When he was bringing me out for a brand new start

I could have turned and run the other way

And been miles from where I am today

I am so glad that he didn't suffer it to be so

I am so grateful that He knew what I didn't know!

Yes, it could have been me, yet attempting to make things in my life turn out right

But I'm so glad that I finally yielded and gave up the fight!

#Trust and Obey

Nugget #56
Next In Line

Next in line to receive
An abundant harvest reaped from a planted seed

It's your turn, it's your time
To move up to the front of the line

You have held up the rear long enough
You waited patiently even when times were tough

Steadfastness pays off, just you wait and see
Fervent prayers are answered eventually!

#Pray Without Ceasing

Nugget #57
Truly Blessed

What does it mean to be truly blessed?
Is it about enjoying a life of only peace and rest?

Or is it about having all the things about which you
have dreamed?
And never having to worry about anything ever again?

Life is not always calm and it doesn't promise that we
won't face any harm or storms

But through it all, if we are able to say,
"With God's help I can make it another day"

…Then that is truly a blessing!

#Too Blessed To Be Stressed

Nugget #58
I Am Blessed

I am blessed to be able to lift my voice and say
Thank you Lord for another day

I am blessed to have eyes to see
That my God is yet leading and guiding me

I am blessed to have ears to hear
That He is yet whispering, "I Am Near"

I am blessed to have feet to go
To someone who needs to know
That they too are blessed!

#Share Your Blessings

Nugget #59
God's Mercy

Never leave home without it
Never ever doubt it

Never forget to thank Him for it
Always remember to ask the Lord, will you have mercy

Never neglect to show it
And it will come back to you doubled

It will follow you all the days of your life
Bringing goodness right along by its side!

#Lord Have Mercy

Nugget #60
A Wealthy Place

Why won't you please come with me?
To a wealthy place and I think you will agree

That it is a most outstanding sanctuary
Overflowing with peace, love, and tranquility

Nothing broken, marred, or disfigured
But oh my is it gracefully situated

I know it's so hard to imagine such a place
When you consider the path that it takes to get there

So many ups and downs and turn arounds
And a whole lot of rocky ground

But if you can just stay on track
And never think about going back

You will reach your destination!

Where in the world, you might ask, could this place be?
My sisters and brothers that place is ME!

Silver and gold have I none
But a wealth of peace, love, and a heap of wisdom ob-
tained from the race of life I have run
You wouldn't believe what I've been through and where
I've come from!

#Looking Back Over My Life

Nugget #61
Amazing Grace

It takes amazing grace to run this race

No amount of exercise will win this prize

It's not about what you do or do not eat
Or trying to avoid the agony of defeat

It's not about building muscles, or countless hours of training
But loving not this world requires amazing restraining

All you need to do to really start
Is to love the Lord with all your heart

And He will make sure that you finish
Because by His Amazing Grace we are already winners!

Nugget #62
I Can't

I can't turn a frown upside down
But I know someone who can

I can't change a season of falling down into a season of
springing forward in life
But I know someone who can

I can't believe that He died on the cross for me
But He Did!

#So Glad That Jesus Can Do What I Can't

Nugget #63
Planting

Planting seeds brings an abundant harvest
With barns filled with plenty and enough for tomorrow

Planting love brings a stockpile of peace
Hearts bursting from the seams with sweet relief!

#Hearts Filled With Love Leave No Room For Anything Else

Nugget #64
From The Inside Out

Things are not as they always seem
It is not always what it looks like

Without a doubt, most things begin from the inside
out
That mysterious place we often do not think much
about

The inside of one's mind, the inside of one's soul
We often wonder…if only the truth could be told

A smile is made on a face
But did it come from a truly happy place?

But oh if we could turn that smile inside out and search
everywhere

We may just find out that that smile was never really
there!
So ask God to teach you to look at and love people
from the inside out!

Nugget #65
More Than Enough

More than enough tears have been shed
We could use a lot more laughter instead

More than enough sleepless nights
Stressing over battles of life that we're trying to fight

More than enough bad news reports
Talking about this, that, and the other

But God has more than enough solutions to all of our problems!

#Jesus Is The Answer

Nugget #66
God Has Done It Again

If He did it before, He can and will do it again

My God has never run out of plans

To bring you out to take you up

He's always pouring out blessings into your cup!

Nugget #67
Our Steps Are Ordered

Dreams that don't come true
Plans that never follow through

Relationships that took a turn for the worse
Loans and investments that were not reimbursed

Promises that were not kept
Hopes and desires that went sour and not right but left

Is it all in vain, you may ask yourself....the answer is
NO, because our steps are ordered by the Lord!

God orders mourning before comfort, hunger and
thirst before being filled, calamity before mercy...be-
cause He knows that it is a menu of life that all works
together for our good.

Many things that He orders for us are not good to us,
but they are certainly GOOD FOR US!

Let Him order for you, He knows what's best.

Enjoy your meal of life that God orders and you will
always come back for more!

#Y'all Come Back Now

Nugget #68
Enough Is Enough

Enough is Enough, because you see, they are identical twins. When you get one, you get the other. They are double trouble, double heartache, and double pain. So, you see, that is why you always get more than what you bargained for!

But on the flip side, they have a way of making sure that you get double for your trouble and gain for your pain. And when they are gone, after keeping you up all night, you will get Joy In The Morning.

#Hold On

Nugget #69
Sick and Tired

Based on a True Story

Sick and Tired are co-workers. They have worked together for some time now.

I don't care how bad the economy is, they are never out of employment. As a matter of fact, they do their best work when someone else is out of a job or battling an extended illness, family problems, or any other serious life crisis!

Usually Sick will work a night shift because he specializes in keeping people up all night with pain, heartaches, worry or anything that will cause them not to get a good night's rest.

Then of course, Tired takes over in the morning because he loves to work when people are exhausted from Sick keeping them up all night doing his job!

If you were to take a survey, I am sure that you will find out that there is not a single person alive who has not worked with these guys sometime in their lifetime!

In spite of the fact that they always keep a job, it is mostly part-time jobs as opposed to permanent ones!

The reason for this is that most people eventually get sick and tired of Sick and Tired and fire them. So, they end up packing up and moving on to seek other employment!

Nugget #70
Pain Wrapped In A Gift Box

Some gifts in life that you may receive
When you open them up you can hardly believe

Because the gift inside does not match the wrapping
For you see the gift inside is tattered, worn out and torn
But the box it came out of was beautifully adorned

Which reminds me of the saying, "You can't judge a book by its cover,"
Because pain wrapped in a gift box is like none other!

#To Look At Some People You Won't Believe What They Are Going Through

Nugget #71
Priceless

How much are you willing to pay
For the blessing of living to see another day?

What would it really cost
To recapture love that was once lost?

How much are you willing to spend
For a once in a lifetime chance to begin again?

If you were to check the tag on any of these items, you
would find them marked PRICELESS!

Nugget #72
This Is Not The End

This is not the end of that moment when
You felt that you were the happiest that you had ever
been

This is not the end of when you thought you were at
your best
Ready to tackle any challenge and pass any test

This is not the end but only the beginning
For something that you never imagined is just about to
happen!

#Something Good Is Going To Happen To You

Nugget #73
A Helping Hand

There is nothing in this world like a helping hand

From someone who cares and truly understands

A hand right there to help lift you up and brush you off

After you have stumbled blindly in life's wind-blown dust

A hand to hold you through your darkest nights

To reassure you that it will be alright

Where would you be if it wasn't for those helping hands

Sent by God to make sure that we can stand!

#Help Is On The Way

Nugget #74
Where Have You Been

Peace, my friend, where have you been?
It has been quite a long time since you paid me a visit,
so come on in

I've thought about you often, and I've waited patiently
for you to return
Even though I have had many disturbances
I was sure that you would soon come

I looked just about everywhere
Confusion tried to convince me that you no longer
cared

But I decided to cast those thoughts aside
And lo and behold soon after that you arrived!

Nugget #75
Up And At It

Time to get up and at it
Clock is a-ticking and time is a-passing

You have nursed those wounds long enough
It didn't kill ya, just made you tough

So, get on up and dust yourself off
So much more of life to live and lessons to learn!

#Wisdom Humor

Nugget #76
Sleep

Sleep is such a wonderful thing
Preparing for rest and a time to dream

When you've spent so many hours lying awake weeping
Oh what a blessed relief when you find yourself sleep-
ing

Joy comes in the morning but not before sleep!

#A Good Night Sleep Makes A Good Morning
#Rest In The Lord

Nugget #77
Compassion

Compassion is so passionate about making sure that
others' well-being is placed above one's own. Com-
passion shows up when you are all alone and hurting.
It makes you feel like you are more important than
anything else in the world. It gives you its undivided
attention and sees to it that you are fully recovered and
back on your feet!

#Show Some Compassion
#Showing Compassion To Others Will Make You Feel
Better

82

Nugget #78
A Portrait of Happiness

If I were to paint a portrait of happiness, I think I would start by choosing a smile as the paintbrush. For my colors, I would use lots of love, splashes of joy, shades of peace, and an assortment of kindness! Then I would sign it, Patience! Finally, I would look for the perfect frame to compliment such a masterpiece. Yes, you guessed right, I think my life would perfectly frame such a lovely Portrait of Happiness!

Nugget #79
God Ain't Done Yet

You've been through test after test
And you have done your very best
                But
God Ain't Done Yet!

You've prayed and you've prayed
Tried your very best to behave
                But
God Ain't Done Yet!

You may ask yourself, what else must I do
Before I make it through?
How much more do I have to endure?

Remember God has a plan that we sometimes don't
understand

Eyes have not seen, ears have not heard
He has already told us in His Word that

                He Ain't Done Yet!

#Wait Patiently

Nugget #80
God Will Take Care of You

God will take care of you

He said it in His word, He cannot lie, it's really true

And to make you feel really secure

He has angels always watching over you

Two of them called Grace and Mercy

When you need them they will be there in a hurry

Another thing that I love about my God is that he never makes a mistake

Plus He's always on time and never ever late!

Nugget #81
Let It Go

Let go of that ego and foolish pride
That causes you to want to run away and hide

For you see you will never be able to outrun you
So, let me just tell you what you oughta do

Let go of all of those negative thoughts in your head
Of what she said, he said, and they said

I promise you if you just let it go
After a while you won't even think about it anymore!

#Let It Go

Nugget #82
Follow The Instructions

"Follow The Instructions" is posted on just about everything and everywhere

Yet we walk right pass or just ignore it as if it wasn't there

These words, they have great purpose whether you realize it or not

We need to take the time to see what they're all about

For even we were born in this world

With instructions and they are written in God's word

So, you need to read your Bible every day and do exactly what it says

It's a matter of life or death that you trust and obey!

#Read The Bible

Nugget #83
Go and Sin No More

Go and sin no more is a warning that we often ignore

Because we take God's grace and mercy for granted

So, we continue to take chances with sinning until it becomes a bad habit

Just because you don't pay right away

Does not mean that your sins won't catch up with you one day

So, my friend please take heed to this warning

Nothing is worth going to hell for and forever and ever burning!

Nugget #84
Medicine

Medicine comes in more than a bottle or a pill

There are many ways to make someone feel better when they are ill

Sometimes medicine comes in a hug, just holding someone tight without uttering a word

Medicine formulated with love is the world's best prescription

It can bring instant healing and even miracles for any condition!

#Give A Dose Of Love

Nugget #85
Miracles Happen

Miracles happen that's for sure
Miracles are God doing for us what nobody else can do

So, don't let anyone make you believe otherwise
God has one with your name on it that will take you by surprise!

#Your Miracle Is On The Way

Nugget #86
I Feel It On My Knees

When I get down to pray on my knees

I begin to feel amazing relief

It feels so good to talk to my God in prayer

Knowing that when I get up I can leave my burdens right there

It's on my knees that I start to feel brand new

And when I get up I feel so good that I know just what to do!

Nugget #87
I'm In Love

I'm in love with somebody

And let me tell you that He loves me like no other
His love for me surpasses the love of my very own
mother

I'm in love with somebody who loves me uncondition-
ally
Every day when I wake up He has new mercies pre-
pared for me

He even gives me breakfast in bed
When I wake up and pray for my daily bread

I love Him so much with all my heart soul and mind
He is truly one of a kind

I'm in love with His body that shed His very own blood
just for me
And turned around and gave His life on Calvary

By His stripes I am healed
You can't imagine how that makes me feel!

#Thank You Jesus

Nugget #88
Today Is The Best Day

Today is the best day to tell God thank you for all He has done

From early in the morning until the setting of the sun

For tomorrow is not promised so why not take advantage of today

To let God know that He is the best thing that ever happened to you!

Nugget #89
Try This At Home

The next time you find yourself feeling down and home alone

Think about and burst out with a happy song

Let me just warn you that before you know it

You will hear the sound of clapping

It's just your hands starting to feel so good that they joined in together

And just in case you can't carry a tune in a paper cup,

Try this at home first for better results!

Nugget #90
The Lord's Hand

The Lord's Hand just put His signature
On a set of plans designed to bless you
He's sending it express from Heaven by an Angel
And it reads: Always Protect From All Hurt, Harm, or
Danger!

#The Angels Of The Lord Encampeth Round Us

Nugget #91
I'm Still Holding On

I'm still holding on to that thought in my mind that
keeps me focused. I'm holding on to that song in my
heart that makes me happy. I'm holding on to words
that were spoken that keep me encouraged. I'm hold-
ing on to those prayers that have been answered. I'm
still holding on to everything that keeps me holding on!

Nugget #92
Still Dancing

Wisdom helps me to get where I want to be in life.
Dancing helps me to get there faster! I'm leaping, I'm
prancing, I'm still dancing!!!

#Praise God In Advance With A Dance

PART THREE - SOMETHING TO THINK ABOUT!

Nugget #93
Only A Memory

All that I truly used to miss no longer exists
All that is really left is lingering memories of what I
thought was once good and best

Don't mistake lingering memories for an opportunity
for a second chance to go back to something that no
longer exists!

– Something To Think About –

#new normals

Nugget #94
When I Think About IT

When I think about IT, whatever IT may be,
I only want to experience feelings that bring healing
internally!

Nugget #95
What's On Your Mind!

So much to do, places to go, people to meet
What's on your mind

What to eat, traffic to beat
People's minds are everywhere, I do declare!

More seriously, wondering what will become of me
Yet another decision to make concerning purpose and
destiny

That is what stays on my mind!

Nugget #96
Stinking Thinking

Don't make it worse than it really is

It's not always as bad as it feels

What you're thinking can be deceiving

Be very careful about what you start believing

Let the peace of God take control of your mind

And leave all that stinking thinking behind!

Nugget #97
Overwhelmed With Amazement

A blink of the eye, the nod of the head
It's so amazing

Being able to swallow a morsel of bread
It's so amazing

To be able to pen these words to paper
Is truly amazing

God you are Amazing!

Nugget #98
Second Chance

A second chance does not come by happenstance

It is not something that we should take for granted

For it's not guaranteed or promised

Because what we call a second chance is really God's
Mercy and Grace

Picking us up when we mess up and fall down in this
life's race!

Nugget #99
A Bad Mistake

Sometimes it only takes for you to make one bad mistake
To turn your life upside down

But something good can yet come from it
If you are quick to repent

And truly mean it from your heart

But please remember this

If you, at a later date
Find yourself repeating that same bad mistake

Then it is no longer a bad mistake
But has started to become a fatal habit!

Nugget #100
Satan Is Looking For A Job –
DON'T HIRE HIM

There is a book in the Bible titled Job. It just so happens to be spelled the same as the word job that we all know, but it has a different pronunciation.

– True Story! –

So, Satan was walking up and down in the earth, and ended up going to God inquiring about a job.

God recommends Job, who had the credentials and qualifications to hire him.

Long story short, Satan discovers that the work is much more difficult than he thought it would be and that he is not as qualified for the job as he assumed!

So, the last I heard, Satan is yet walking up and down in the earth, and he yet remains jobless and homeless.

Let's keep him that way!

#He's A Freeloader
#Got Kicked Out Of Heaven

Nugget #101
Dressed Up Lie

Just because you dressed that lie in white
I'm here to tell you that it's still not right

You can douse it with cologne
But the truth is that the lie is still wrong

You may try to slim it down and dress it up in all black
But a lie in any color still looks fat

You see telling lies is out of style
Whether you dress it up in all white or a little black

Once it steps out of your mouth,
You won't be able to take it back

If the truth be told, it's everlasting
Wear it proudly, it's always in fashion!

Nugget #102
STAY FOCUSED!!!

You will never really be successful or accomplish anything if you don't stay focused. Success is not based solely on hard work, education, talent, and skill. You can have all of these and more, but if you do not stay focused, it is like pouring water into a container with holes in it!

STAY FOCUSED!!!

#What Are You Looking At

Nugget #103
Transparency

Your transparency is for others to see
That it is not about what's on the outside but Christ that resides inwardly

No, it's not all about you
But what He has brought you through

He is the one who took you through and brought you out
So others could see and know without a doubt

That He will do the same for them too!

#104
BLACK AND BLUE

Black and Blue are never my favorite colors

When my days are black as midnight from extended stay heartaches

When the circles under my eyes have gone from dark to black from sleepless nights

When I'm battling with shades of depression that are giving me the blues!

Nugget #105
Watch Your Mouth

Everything that comes up does not have to come out
Yes, that's right, I'm talking about your mouth.

Remember your mouth is the safe that secures your words,
And your words are packed with power

That's why you should stand watch over them
Minute by minute and hour by hour

Once those words are released into the atmosphere
I'm mighty afraid of what could appear!

#Sometimes Just Shut Up!

Nugget #106
Leave It Alone

God gave you the strength to walk away

He knew you couldn't survive another day

Now that it's over and what's done is done

Thank God for bringing you out, move on, and leave it alone!

Nugget #107
Once In A Lifetime

Only once in a lifetime do most things come around

You can search for them over and over again but they will no longer be found

Remember life is a training for future reigning

So, practice every day to rule with love, kindness, honesty, and integrity

#Practice Does Make Perfect

Nugget #108
Hell's Fury

Hell's fury is like collecting precious jewelry

You can never be satisfied or get enough even as the collection becomes larger and larger

Nothing in life is worth going there

Make sure you don't add to Hell's Collection of Fury

#Hell Is Hot
#Hot And Forever

Nugget #109
Question Marks

Instead of concentrating so much on looking for answers to questions, you should put more time and energy in asking yourself questions.

Searching for answers only leads to more questions. Asking yourself questions inspires and motivates you to become proactive.

When you ask yourself questions as opposed to looking for answers, you turn question marks into exclamation points!!!

#Get Excited About Life
#Oh Happy Day
#???
#!!!

Nugget #110
When God Clears His Throat

When God clears His throat, somewhere along the way of life you have failed to give Him your undivided attention. It means you have allowed too much distance to come between you and the one who cares for you the most. When God clears His throat, it signifies that He has been leading but we have not been following. He has been showing us signs but we have been ignoring them. When you find that your life is nothing but a bad case of hiccups, it just may be that God is clearing His throat! When God has to clear His throat, it gives us the hiccups!

#Listening To God Cures The Hiccups

Nugget #111
Disobedience

Disobedience has many consequences for which you
only have yourself to blame

Remember if you continue to hit a brick wall
You most certainly will continue to fall

Doing the same wrong thing over and over again
Is simply disobedience my friend

For you see the things in this life that you must do
Are not left entirely up to you

No, my friend you cannot pick and choose
But you must obey all of your Creator's Rules!

Nugget #112
Miracles!

Miracles, miracles and more miracles are waiting on
someone to claim them. They are in the lost and found
in heaven and can be yours by faith for the asking!

#Believe and Receive
#Lost By Unbelief
#Found By Faith
#Yours For The Asking

Nugget #113
An Unplanned Blessing

God has something very special in His hand

Something that you never dreamed of, imagined, or planned

It's a surprise for all that you've been through

He's about to release an awesome unplanned blessing to you!

#Surprise, Surprise

Nugget #114
It's No Secret

It is no secret that we all desire to receive love
From someone truly special and be the recipient of

If it's no secret then why do we spend
So much time trying to keep it hid, locked up in
A heart that is longing to give and receive?

Why aren't we spreading it all around
Instead of making it difficult to be found?

Yes, what the world needs more of is plain ole love

It's no secret that there's just not enough of it

#Spread the Love
#The Secret Is Out

Nugget #115
No More Chains

No more chains or any evidence
That there was ever any entanglement

No bruises or scars
Or distorted memories in the heart

You wouldn't even believe that a life of trouble once had
me bound
'Cause there ain't no more chains to be found!

#Freedom

Nugget #116
Been There, Done That

Ever since Been There and Done That became best friends, they have formed a bond like none other. It is like a soul tie that is almost impossible to disconnect.

You see, Been There and Done That have so much in common. They have both had very similar, and even sometimes the very same, let-downs and challenges of life.

Their experiences not only taught them what to do but also what not to do as well. But most importantly, they both realized that they came out a whole lot wiser, stronger, and better because they had BEEN THERE AND DONE THAT!

Now they both want a t-shirt…those two…

#Inseparable
#BFFs

Nugget #117
When Silence Speaks

When silence speaks, it's best to listen
And try to comprehend why sounds and words are missing

It may be a warning
A sign or something really alarming

Please pay close attention when silence speaks!

Nugget #118
Can You Hear Me Now?

I escaped dangers seen and unseen

Thinking it was just a coincidence

I stumbled up on some circumstances

That I thought just occurred as a result of me taking some risky chances

Seems like I kept running into a brick wall

Only to recover from another fall

Then I began to really wonder Lord why and oh Lord how

And He answered me back and said, "Can you hear me now?"

Nugget #119
When God Turns The Storm To Calm

When God turns your storms into calm
No amount of life's bad weather predictions will make any difference

When God says no to your storms, there won't be any
Only sunshine and clear skies will there be plenty!

#Whose Report Will You Believe

Nugget #120
Just Look At God!

Just look at God and all the great things that He has done

There is nothing too hard for my God

And you just sit back and wait

'Cause you ain't seen nothing yet

Did you know that He will open Heaven's Door?

And then pour you out blessings that you won't have room for

Just keep on planting good seeds

And watch Him supply your every need

And wait a minute, did I tell you that He will open doors that nobody can shut

And in amazement you can just look at God while He's doing all of that!

Nugget #121
A Love-Filled Heart

A heart filled with love is a storage packed with warm
and tender awards

Looking and searching for countless recipients in which
to impart

The world would be a much better place

If there were more hearts filled with love

Instead of hearts full of cold and empty space!

Nugget #122
Haters and Elevators

You want to know how to overcome your haters

Just get on and press the love button on life's elevator

It will take you from the bottom to the top

You will feel so good inside that you won't want to stop

So, don't let those haters keep you down

Just keep riding that love elevator

And you will get where you are going sooner than those haters!

Nugget #123
Best Behavior

When I was just a little girl I was told
Be on your best behavior, children are to be seen and
not heard

When I became a young lady, the older people said
Do this, don't do that
Be careful young lady how you act

But as I grew older and became wiser I realized that best
behavior is just plain ole
Experience and Knowledge, stumbling over and quar-
reling with each other!

#Humor In Wisdom

Nugget #124
It's Already Done

It's already done
Be not anxious about the setting of the sun

If God said it, you've already won
Just believe and it will never return!

Nugget #125
The Battle of Distraction

The battle of distraction is always picking and starting a fight

Trying to hinder me from doing what is right

Just go somewhere and leave me alone

In Jesus' name go back to where you came from!

Nugget #126
Leave Your Light On!

Don't forget to leave your light on at a moment when you are feeling weak

Don't be so quick to get upset and misjudge someone because they walked right past you and didn't speak

Instead say a little prayer for them because you never know what they might be going through

I believe the Lord would be very pleased if that is what you chose to do

So, remember to leave your light on and always let your light so shine

Your light may be the very one that leads that person to Christ!

Nugget #127
The Power of Experience

Experience is an excellent teacher. When you are fortunate enough to be in its class, pay close attention to each and every lesson. If you do, you will graduate at the top of life's class with honors!

Nugget #128
Don't Turn Around

Don't turn around for fear of what you may see

Something that may cause you to change your destiny

Too many obstacles to entangle your feet

So much to discourage you by chance you could meet

Whatever you do, please don't turn around

You've come too far by faith to not receive your crown!

Nugget #129
Contentment

Contentment means that you are committed to waiting out and making the best of any situation that life brings your way until things change. No matter how negative things may be at the present moment, Contentment will pull up a chair and relax and may even take a nap!

Nugget #130
Sealed With A Kiss

When I close my eyes, to my surprise

I can still see

When I lower the shades down over my eyes

Even in the dark, I experience a romance in my heart

I envision a love affair between my purpose and destiny

That is sealed with a

Kiss of my eyelids!

Nugget #131
Happily Ever After

Happily Ever After is just around the corner of all of life's disasters. It is right next door to the end of it all. Don't worry, you will be there before you know it!

#Don't Worry Be Happy

Nugget #132
I Don't Want To Die

I don't want to die and take any love with me

But I want to leave it all here so that someone else can have plenty

I don't want to die and bury in the earth

Anything that was meant to remain here to live on and give birth

We don't know the day or hour when we are supposed to die

So, let's get busy, grow, and thrive

And do all we can while we're yet alive

So, when we are planted in this earth

Our lives will grow seeds and not just weeds.

Nugget #133
From the Ground Up

Sometimes life will cause you to have to rebuild again

After everything around you has crumbled by life's troublesome storms and winds

Make no mistake about it when your life has fallen apart

You can rebuild again and have a brand new start

You just never know, you may with God's help do much better

From the ground up will turn out something much greater!

Nugget #134
WOW!

Sometimes the only thing I can say is WOW
Because I'm so overwhelmed and I don't know how

How can a God that I've never seen
Be so real to me deep down within?

I hear His voice and feel His love
He pours out blessings that I feel so unworthy of

Even now, all I can say is WOW!

#speechless
#Awed

Nugget #135
Fruit or Gift

If you had your choice between receiving a gift or a piece of fruit which would you choose?

You would probably make a dash for the gift that had bright wrappings, ribbons, and bows

Instead of a lonely piece of fruit sitting over in an old bowl.

But I think I would pick that old piece of fruit because inside of it are seeds that I could plant.

Then that one piece of fruit would later produce a harvest of blessings that one gift can't!

#Don't Despise Humble Beginnings

Nugget #136
Compromise

Compromise will take you by surprise if you don't stand your ground

Everything that you once stood for will soon come tumbling down

Don't make the same mistake that countless others have made

One moment of compromise can take a lifetime to repay!

Nugget #137
Desperation

Desperation will alter your destination

Because it will take you away from your course

Instead of moving forward, you will end up in reverse

What's meant to be, it will be

So, don't become so desperate that you miss your true destiny!

Nugget #138
Sometimes It Hurts

Sometimes in life it hurts to be yourself
Trying hard not to be like everybody else

But let me tell you what hurts even more
Is to miss living the life that you were born in this world for!

#Be Yourself

Nugget #139
Not My Fault

You see it's not my fault
It's just the way that I was taught

To love in spite of, to forgive when you don't under-
stand
To pray for others, even those who have caused you
some pain

It's not my fault but I take the blame
Because you see, the blessings that I received far out-
weighed the suffering and pain

Nugget #140
Crying From The Grave

So many lost souls are crying from the grave
Lord if you only give me one more chance I promise to
behave

But I am sad to say said the Lord, "It's now too late.
You had chance after chance after chance to get it right,
I've already shut Heaven's gate!"

Nugget #141
Birth After Death

There is always something that is birthed after death

Soon after a dream is gone

Another one is sure to be born

It doesn't leave much time for crying and grieving

Something about a birth after a death is really relieving!

Nugget #142
Adversity vs. Prosperity

Some people spend and waste all their life trying to avoid adversity

If they had millions of dollars, they would surely die penniless

Because to live without adversity in this life is an impossibility

True prosperity is learning from adversity how to live the best life you can

In reality there is no prosperity without adversity!

Nugget #143
Beware

Beware lest a temporary place of weakness
Becomes a permanent place of death…separation from
God!

Beware lest your walk by faith become distorted by
what is in your sight!

Beware lest an innocent glimpse becomes a poisonous
stare!

B – Being
E – Extra
W – Watchful
A – Always
R – Resisting
E – Evil

Nugget #144
Kindred Stranger

So many faces we see as we pass along life's way

Rubbing elbows with strangers each and every day

Why do we always see someone who looks so familiar

Even at times it's like looking at yourself in a mirror

Then when I think about it, everyone on this earth has so much in common

Maybe it's because we all have different mothers but we all have the same Heavenly Father!

Nugget #145
Just A Little

After a drought, just a little rain
Can bring about a significant change

Just a little bit of love
Can make a big difference in this huge world

So just a little can go a long way
You can do a lot in twenty-four hours in just one day

It doesn't take a whole lot
Just use the little bit that you got

And if you put that little bit in the Master's Hand
You can sit back and watch that little bit multiply and expand!

Nugget #146
Darker Than Midnight

Something darker than midnight
Is the hour just before the daybreak

The dawning of a new era and the laying to rest
Of some of life's heartaches

Something else darker than midnight
I shutter to think about or imagine

Is a lost soul gone from this earth
Locked in eternal darkness forever after!

Nugget #147
I Ain't Complaining

Lord knows I ain't complaining
About what I been through

'Cause I know it could have been worse
Someone else would have loved to have been in my
shoes

Don't get me wrong
Sometimes it got kinda rough

But I ain't complaining
Because it ended up making me tough!

Nugget #148
Give It Away

I want to give myself away
So that someone else will have a better day

I want to give myself away
So that someone else will be able to say,
"I'm having a wonderful day"

The reason I don't mind giving myself away
Is because it's more blessed to give than to receive!

#Give It Away And It Comes Back Double

Nugget #149
In Memory Of

When I smile, it's in memory of the hardest test of life
that I finally passed.

When I laugh, it's in memory of love that was lost and
then later regained.

When I dance, it's in memory of all the blessings that
are to come!

Nugget #150
A New Beginning

Time to press forward, no more looking back

The past is the past, new opportunities are approaching fast!

A new beginning today will become the past in the future

So, make the best of every day!

PART FOUR - PROVERBS "32", THE READER'S JOURNAL OF WISDOM NUGGETS

Proverbs "32"

Yes, this section of the book is dedicated especially to you, the reader. Those of you who are familiar with the Bible know that there is a book in it titled Proverbs. Proverbs is known as the book of wisdom because it is packed with divinely-inspired wisdom nuggets. But as some of you may also know, this book only contains 31 chapters.

No, I am not by any means adding to the Bible, but I am providing you an opportunity to begin journaling your own chapter of wisdom nuggets. Actually, this is how this book started out, with me journaling my own nuggets.

Perhaps after absorbing all of the 150 nuggets in Live to Learn and Learn to Live, you would like to pen down some precious treasures that you have discovered throughout your treasure hunt!

Allow Proverbs "32" to become your personal treasure

chest of priceless nuggets from your heart! From time to time you will be able to go back and delight in all of the riches that you have received from living to learn and learning to live!

You are now even wiser and you can finish out your life happily and productively. I know you have been greatly inspired as a result of reading this book. I know I have been even as I was writing it!

So, go ahead and begin penning your own wisdom nuggets so that you can become deeply appreciative of what life has taught you.

This is your Proverbs "32!"

My Personal Wisdom Journal

_____

_____

_____

_____

_____

_____

_____

_____

_____

_____

_____

_____

_____

_____

_____

_____

_____

_____

_____

_____

_____

My Personal Wisdom Journal

My Personal Wisdom Journal

_____

_____

_____

_____

_____

_____

_____

_____

_____

_____

_____

_____

_____

_____

_____

_____

_____

_____

My Personal Wisdom Journal

_____

_____

_____

_____

_____

_____

_____

_____

_____

_____

_____

_____

_____

_____

_____

_____

_____

_____

My Personal Wisdom Journal

_____

_____

_____

_____

_____

_____

_____

_____

_____

_____

_____

_____

_____

_____

_____

_____

_____

_____

_____

My Personal Wisdom Journal

_____

_____

_____

_____

_____

_____

_____

_____

_____

_____

_____

_____

_____

_____

_____

_____

_____

My Personal Wisdom Journal

_____

_____

_____

_____

_____

_____

_____

_____

_____

_____

_____

_____

_____

_____

_____

_____

_____

_____

_____

_____

_____

My Personal Wisdom Journal

My Personal Wisdom Journal

_____

_____

_____

_____

_____

_____

_____

_____

_____

_____

_____

_____

_____

_____

_____

_____

_____

_____

_____

My Personal Wisdom Journal

_____

_____

_____

_____

_____

_____

_____

_____

_____

_____

_____

_____

_____

_____

_____

_____

_____

_____

_____

_____

CPSIA information can be obtained
at www.ICGtesting.com
Printed in the USA
FFOW02n0720160518
46680048-48797FF